Feb. 25, 1955

Leila C. Fry

Marie F. Fox

The Tabernacle
in the Wilderness

The Tabernacle
in the Wilderness

BY CHARLES E. FULLER

Edited by
Grace L. and Daniel P. Fuller

FLEMING H. REVELL COMPANY

Dedicated to the radio friends
Whose prayers and offerings
Through the years
Have made it possible for us
To minister
To so many in far-away, lonely places.

FOREWORD

IN THE EARLIEST DAYS OF MR. FULLER'S PREPARATION for the ministry, it was his burning desire and constant prayer that he might be able to reach with the Gospel the people in the neglected places, the lonely ones who had no chance to go to church—no opportunities to attend Bible conferences and no one to point them to the Lamb of God Who taketh away the sin of the world.

How marvelously God answered that prayer, above all that my husband could ask or *think*, for there were no radio programs in 1920! Very soon after they came on the scene, he became deeply impressed with the possibilities of using this new medium for sending far and wide the good news of salvation.

Then one night, in a berth on a train speeding from Philadelphia to Chicago, a burden of prayer came down on my husband, and God clearly revealed to him that he should undertake a Gospel program by radio. Feeling entirely inadequate, he shrank from the task, but God continued to lay the burden on his heart. Very soon after returning

7

to California, he took steps to buy time on one small station in Santa Ana. That was in 1925, and it marked the beginning which led eventually to the world coverage of the greatly loved Old-Fashioned Revival Hour. How gracious God has been to grant Dr. Fuller thirty continuous years of preaching the Gospel by radio!

As we look back over those blessed years of growth, we see a rugged, uphill path, with many obstacles in the way which, in our own strength, would have been insurmountable. But the light of God's goodness, mercy, and faithfulness has shown over every step of the way! Satan's opposition has been very real over the years, for isn't he the prince of the power of the air? And hasn't the Gospel been going out through *His* realm? Ah yes, Satan is powerful, and he did his best to hinder and block at every turn. But God is *all-powerful,* and He certainly helped us times without number, encouraging and comforting His own.

Even during the depression years there was steady growth in the number of stations, because of the faithfulness of Christians who were willing to sacrifice where there was often so little to give, in order to extend the radio coverage and reach more listening ears. God bless those faithful radio friends and supporters!

Eternity alone will reveal the great number of souls who will be in Glory because, as they sat by their radios, the Holy Spirit showed them their need of salvation. People in the loneliest places have heard of God's great love for them; homesteaders out on the desert or up in the lonely canyons; trappers, and people snowbound in far-away cabins. The bed-ridden have had months and years of suffering lightened by the sermons from the Word of God. We have had letters from people in lighthouses where for weeks they could not get ashore, but through the winds and lashing rain have heard the lovely voices singing, "What a Friend We Have in Jesus." "No, Never Alone," and many other grand old Gospel hymns.

Our service men have listened through two wars, having a touch of home though far away, and many have written that the Hour has also kept them in touch with God and helped them resist temptations. One service man wrote that he and two others were trekking through a jungle, they stopped to rest and there, turning on a small radio, caught a long-familiar voice and heard Dr. Fuller praying for "God's blessing on our boys in the service, wherever they are." He wrote, "The tears sure flowed that day." Men in prison cells listen regularly; the lepers listen and ask us to keep our music cheery; we have heard from a brothel, from a young girl who grew up in a Christian home; and in many cocktail lounges the program is tuned in every Sunday!

Though the Old-Fashioned Revival Hour

9

reaches Britain from eleven to twelve midnight over Radio Luxembourg, yet there is a tremendous and most appreciative listening audience there, and we receive letters telling of blessing and conversions among all classes of persons. One letter from a man in Wales particularly impressed us: "In our valley, where the miners work so hard, we see on Thursday nights lights in the windows of many houses, where they wait up late to hear of Him Who is the Light of the World." A trapper wrote, "Anyone passing would wonder to hear such organ music and such singing coming out of my shack!" An old lady living alone wrote: "You come with your lovely singers and the organ and piano music right into my poor little room every week, and it is like the music of the angels." I could tell you of many, many more who listen on other continents and under greatly differing circumstances.

We have had many requests for copies of these sermons on "The Tabernacle in the Wilderness." Now, here they are in this book which we have tried to keep as nearly similar as possible to Mr. Fuller's style of speaking. They are sent out with a prayer that they may be of even greater blessing than when given over the radio.

GRACE PAYTON FULLER
San Marino, Calif.

CONTENTS

CONTENTS

The Tabernacle
in the Wilderness

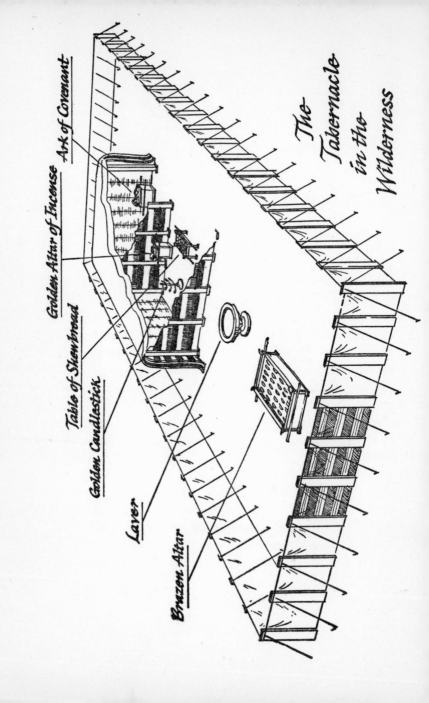

The Tabernacle in the Wilderness

Ark of Covenant

Golden Altar of Incense

Table of Shewbread

Golden Candlestick

Laver

Brazen Altar

CHAPTER I

The Tabernacle in the Wilderness

FRIENDS, AS WE BEGIN THIS SOUL SATISFYING, HEART thrilling study of "The Tabernacle in the Wilderness," may the Psalmist's prayer constantly be ours, "Lord, open thou mine eyes that I may behold wondrous things out of thy law." I trust that when we have finished this series you will have fallen in love, as I did many years ago, with this rich teaching—which, in the Old Testament foreshadows the Christ of the New Testament, and shows the way by which a sinful man may approach and have fellowship with a holy God.

IMPORTANCE OF THIS STUDY

This study of the Book of Exodus, and particularly the Tabernacle, is a spiritual "eye opener" and I can testify, after years of meditating on this portion of God's Word, that the one who lets the Holy

Spirit enlighten him, understanding this teaching in its fullness, will never be led astray into false cults, but will be sure that no man cometh unto the Father except through Christ.

The Bible tells us that all have sinned; the natural man is dead in trespasses and sins. The supreme question of all ages, far above any political question, national or international, is this: how can a sinful man, by nature fallen—how can such a one approach a holy God? Man needs God. How can he find Him? How can he be acceptable before Him? How can he know forgiveness of sin, be at peace with God, and have fellowship with Him? The teaching of the Tabernacle in the Wilderness shows us the answer. For, if a soul now laden with sin, in whose heart there is no peace, will approach God in His way, in the way as shown in the Tabernacle, he will be forgiven, reconciled, and will become a new creature fitted to fellowship with the Holy God. The Tabernacle shows forth in types the glorious gospel of Christ which is the power of God unto salvation to everyone who believeth.

Any who will diligently study this marvelous pre-picture of our Lord Jesus Christ will have the eyes of his understanding opened to spiritual truths, and his hunger and thirst after righteousness will be satisfied. As he studies he will grow in knowledge of our Lord, becoming steadfast in his faith, unmovable amidst the storms, stress, and turmoil of life. He will find increasingly sweet fellowship with God, and though his paths be rough, he will be sustained, kept steady, and at peace on the wilderness journey in this world and to heaven itself.

CHRIST IS THE KEY TO THE BIBLE

First of all, let us consider some basic truths relative to the Word of God. The main subject in the Bible from the beginning of Genesis through Revelation is none other than the Lord Jesus Christ. The eternal God exhausts the resources of human language to tell forth the wonders, the grace, the mercy, and compassionate love God has for all men everywhere. He uses as illustrations the material things round about us, things with which we are familiar, to better enable us to understand that His Son is the Mediator, the One and Only Way that sinful man can approach a sinless God. The furnishings of the Tabernacle which we shall study in detail later are used to show us God's way of approach to Himself. Jesus is the Brazen Altar, Jesus is the Laver, Jesus is the Shewbread, Jesus is the Light of the World, Jesus is the Altar of Incense. He is the blood-sprinkled Mercy Seat in the Holy of Holiness. No man cometh, I say again, *No man cometh unto the Father but by Jesus Christ!*

Now notice Exodus 25:8. The children of Israel had been in bondage and slavery in Egypt. God called Moses to lead His people out of captivity to

17

the Promised Land. The first twelve chapters of Exodus record the terrible sufferings of that bondage and God's deliverance. We are told of the beginning of that long journey, when God led His people, some one million five-hundred-thousand of them, with their cattle and personal goods, out of Egypt by the way of the Red Sea, by the waters of Marah, by the wells of Elim. God led the Israelites, His children, across the desert waste to a camping place at the foot of Mount Sinai. Then, according to the 25th chapter, verse 8, when Moses was upon the mountain, God spoke to him and said, ". . . let them make me a sanctuary; that I may dwell among them." Then God gave Moses detailed instructions concerning the construction of that sanctuary which was called the Tabernacle in the Wilderness. When that Tabernacle was finished—parts of it made of wood overlaid with gold—God came down and dwelt there in the midst of His people. Wood speaks forth the Lord's humanity, and gold speaks of His Deity.

Centuries later, long after dwelling in their midst during the Wilderness journey, the Lord God Jehovah came down from the Glory above to be born of a virgin. He came down and dwelt among men in a body of flesh and bones; He was God manifest in the flesh. We turn to John 1:14 and we read ". . . the Word [that is Christ] was made flesh, and dwelt [i.e., tabernacled] among us." We (i.e., those that have been enlightened as to His glory) we beheld His glory as the only begotten of the Father full of grace and truth." He tabernacled or dwelt among His people in the days of long ago during the Wilderness journey. He is here now in the person of the Holy Spirit to tabernacle among us today, and our bodies are now the temples of the Holy Spirit!

A DESCRIPTION OF THE TABERNACLE

As we study, I ask you to refer frequently to the picture of the Tabernacle in the front of this book, for this will help greatly in your understanding of the teaching.

The Tabernacle was some forty-five feet in length, and about fifteen feet in width; the rear end and two sides were made of boards, each board about fifteen feet in height by two inches in thickness. The Tabernacle stood in a courtyard surrounded by curtains of fine, white, pure linen, some eight and one-half feet high, enclosing an area of 175 feet in length and eighty-seven and one-half feet in width.

The entrance, which was on the east side of this courtyard, was closed by a curtain of fine-twined linen in blue, purple and scarlet. Let us pause a moment to consider how purple is made. Blue and red are mixed to make purple. Blue, the blue of heaven, speaks of Christ's deity. The scarlet speaks of earth, and the two together picture for us the deity and humanity of Christ our Mediator.

Note the order and arrangement of the articles of furniture in the courtyard and in the Tabernacle itself. First, at the one entrance was the Brazen Altar upon which the sacrifice of a spotless lamb was burning continually. Next was the Laver at which the priest washed his hands and feet; then, entering into the Holy Place at the right was the Table of Shewbread, and on the left was the Golden Candlestick. Just before the entrance to the Holy of Holies was the Altar of Incense. In the Holy of Holies stood the Ark of the Covenant, the blood-sprinkled Mercy Seat and the Overshadowing Cherubim.

Now note, the articles of furniture are placed in the shape of a cross—the main shaft was made by the Brazen Altar, the Laver, the Altar of Incense, and the Ark of the Covenant; the Table of Shewbread and the Candlestick made the two arms. Thus, in the beginning we see the Cross, and we are taught that the basis of all our hope for time and eternity is the Cross of Calvary! No wonder Paul, writing to the Corinthians, said, "I am determined to know nothing among you, save Jesus Christ and him crucified." No wonder we sing "In the Cross of Christ I Glory"—"We Must Need Go Home by the Way of the Cross"—"Near the Cross" and "The Old Rugged Cross."

NEW TESTAMENT COUNTERPARTS

Now, let us leave the Old Testament briefly, and with your Bibles open let us look into the Gospel of John. Perhaps it never occurred to you that the order of approach to God on the part of sinful man, as outlined in the Tabernacle, is beautifully shown in the Gospel of John. Will you note in chapter one, verse twenty-nine that John the Baptist said one day ". . . Behold, the Lamb of God, which taketh away the sin of the world." This most certainly points back to the sacrifice on the Brazen Altar. And let me say this to you (and remember it if you never hear my voice again) that you will never become cleansed of sin and have fellowship with a Holy God unless you have come to the Cross, the Brazen Altar where the Lamb was slain! There and there only is the sin question settled! I know that there are thousands of people in the various cults today who are trying to have fellowship with God—trying to find Him. Listen. They never can come to God and have forgiveness, peace and fellowship, until they have come to the Cross—repenting, and confessing their need of a Saviour! Get it, please, and remember that John 1:29 points back to the Brazen Altar in the Tabernacle in the Wilderness. Mark that verse in your Bible, and write beside it "The Brazen Altar."

Then, as to the Laver for washing. There are

three references to water in the first five chapters of John. First to the waterpots at the wedding in Cana of Galilee. In chapter 4:14, "but whosoever drinketh the water that I shall give him shall never thirst; but the water that I shall give him shall be in him a well of water springing up into everlasting life." In chapter five we have the scene at the pool of Bethesda. All these references speak of various aspects of the washing or cleansing with water and hark back to the Laver which was beyond the Brazen Altar. Then in John 6 we come to the feeding of the five-thousand which is the great discourse on the Bread of Life. In John 8:12 Jesus said, ". . . I am the light of the world . . ." which speaks of the Golden Candlestick. Then in the 17th chapter of John we have our Great High Priest's prayer, Jesus at the Altar of Incense, and, brother, listen to me, your prayers cannot be heard and be acceptable unto God until first you pass the Brazen Altar—the Lamb slain—until you are cleansed through His Word, and until you have fed upon the Bread of Life and walked in the light of His Word. After this your prayers will be answered! But remember, God says that if we regard iniquity in our hearts, He will not hear us. He also says, "Who shall ascend up to the Holy Mount? Those who have clean hands and a pure heart." He has provided for us His method of cleansing. We must come in His way.

Now notice, in the Book of Romans. Oh, I want you to fall in love with the teaching of the Tabernacle in both the Old and the New Testaments. It is so rich! Paul writing in Romans, chapters 1 to 3:20, tells of three types of sinners. There is the scarlet, deeply-ingrained sinner, the evil man. Then Paul speaks of the man who feels that because he is a moral man his own works of righteousness will make him acceptable before God. Paul speaks last of the religious man, the one who is faithful to his duties to the church, but who never has experienced the new birth. He sums it up by saying, ". . . all have sinned and come short . . . !" Then in Romans 3:21-25, Paul shows there is a way for sinful man to come to God by the grace which is ours in Christ Jesus; that Christ paid the penalty for our sins, that He was the burnt offering sacrifice which provides man's approach to a Holy God. Read this portion of Scripture over and over again and rejoice, friend of mine, that Christ paid our debt for sin—yours and mine, and through Him we can come boldly to God as our Father. Then in Romans, chapters 6, 7 and 8, we are told we must wash at the Laver in order to enter the Holy Place, and feed upon the Bread, and walk in the Light. Yes, indeed, Paul is pointing back to the Tabernacle. Then, in chapters 12-16 he shows us that as a result of this cleansing we bring forth the fruit of righteousness.

THE ONE WAY OF APPROACH

Now, friends, here is an interesting point. When God gave the instructions to Moses for building the Tabernacle, he first spoke of the Ark of the Covenant where God dwelt, and then of the Brazen Altar, which depicts God coming to man. But when man comes to God he comes by the one gate of entrance, then on to the Brazen Altar and then finally into the Holy of Holies! Yes, God so loved the world that He provided this way of approach to Himself through the one door, Christ Jesus. Have you come by the Table of Shewbread which depicts Christ the Bread of Life, and by the Candlestick which shows Christ interceding for us in prayer? This path leads to the Holy of Holies, to the blood-sprinkled Mercy Seat where a sinner, cleansed, can meet God in fellowship. How clear! How blessed! Do you see it, friend of mine? Oh, may the Holy Spirit, the Great Teacher, open your eyes to behold the wonders of the Book. May you not be indifferent! May you study and become grounded in the Word, not tossed to and fro like children—listening and following any attractive voice. Remember, "There is a way that seemeth right unto a man but the end thereof is the way of death." Come by His way!

Yes, if you come by faith, God will accept you. He will cast your sins behind His back, never to remember them against you, forever. Take God at

His word. That sin question must be settled, either the sinner must die for his sin or an innocent substitute die in his place. Jesus came and died for you, He gave His life a ransom for you (John 1:12). Oh! friends of the radio audience, which is scattered across the nations of earth, how many today will kneel wherever you are, and look up into the Father's face and say, "Oh, God save me, I believe." God will hear you. As we bring this blessed hour to a close, how many here in this visible audience will raise their hands and say, "Brother Fuller, I need Christ as Saviour. I want to be remembered in prayer. I want to receive Him and make Him Lord of my life." Will you raise your hand thus indicating your need of God? Yes, I see hands going up all over. God bless you—Yes, I see you, service man, another service man—anywhere—up in the balcony. I can't acknowledge all of them. Putting your hand up you say, "Brother Fuller, pray for me, I need Christ." We must close in a few seconds, and we shall be praying for you as we have our altar service here. Please continue in prayer as we leave the air. This is Charles E. Fuller saying, "Goodbye, and God's richest blessing upon you."

CHAPTER II

The Curtains of the Tabernacle

Now, with your Bible open to the 25th chapter of Exodus, verse 22, we shall start on a personally conducted tour, down across the peninsula of Sinai to Mount Sinai. The Holy Spirit will be our guide. We leave the arm of the Red Sea and travel eastward to Marah, where the children of Israel found the waters so bitter that they could not drink. There Moses cast a tree into the bitter waters, and they became sweet and refreshing. There is a lesson here for us: in any experience of life the bitterness can be changed and sweetened because of our relation to God through the Cross. We travel on down to Elim where there are wells of water, and where the children of Israel were refreshed in the shade of the palm trees. From Elim we go across the vast desert sands, dry and hot in the daytime, and we finally come to Mount Sinai, a prominent mountain standing some 6,700 feet in elevation.

THE VIEW FROM SINAI

The Holy Spirit directs us up on the side of the mountain where He points out some things of great interest to us. Here on the mountain side we look out over a vast encampment—many hundreds and hundreds of black-topped tents—as far as the eye can see. Our guide tells us that the twelve tribes of Israel are encamped at the foot of the mountain, tribe by tribe in an orderly fashion, beautifully arranged around a central meeting place. Someone in the party suggests that there might be a hundred and forty-four thousand in each tribe. This is merely a suggestion. If we multiply 144,000 by 12, we will have one million five-hundred thousand, or about the number that went on the exodus out of Egypt unto Mount Sinai.

As we stand looking down from the mountain slope, our guide calls our attention to the Tabernacle which is closed in by white linen curtains, and which stands in the very midst of the great encampment of black-topped tents. He impresses us with the fact that inside that court or enclosure is the Brazen Altar upon which the sacrifice is burning continually. Beyond the Brazen Altar is the Laver, at which the priest washes his hands and feet daily before he goes into the Holy Place, there to partake of the bread upon the Table of Shewbread and to trim the lamps of the seven-fold Candlestick. These things he does before he goes to the Altar of Incense for prayer. Furthermore, the Holy Spirit tells us that upon one day in the year, the Day of Atonement, Aaron the High Priest, goes into the Holy of Holies, into the very presence of God, and there he stands before the blood-sprinkled Mercy Seat with the Overshadowing Cherubim. There, on that day, once a year, God's presence is manifested.

Our guide points out the great pillar of cloud which God provided for His children, to guide them by day, to shield them from the hot desert sun, and to become a pillar of fire by night, giving light in the darkness. We can see that great umbrella-like pillar of cloud, standing over the Tabernacle, and as we look we notice that the burning rays of the desert sun do not reach us with such heat, for as it spreads we are partly under the umbrella of that great pillar of cloud. What a good view we have looking out over the vast sea of black tents. Standing there we watch the sun going down in the west and Oh! what a glorious, what an awe-inspiring sight! As the night shadows fall we see that pillar of cloud change and slowly become a pillar of fire! When darkness comes, we see it standing protectively over the acres of black tents, casting a soft, glowing light to illumine God's children in the night time. How sweet, how tender is God's care for His own.

A CLOSER LOOK AT THE TABERNACLE

Now I have told you of this briefly, but I want you to read Exodus 25:22 and then with the Holy Spirit as guide, go down by faith from the mountain-side and approach the Tabernacle. The outer court is some 175 feet in length by eighty-seven and one-half feet in width. "And *there* (will you underline that little word *there* for it's a very important word), and *there* I will meet with thee and will commune with thee."

Now the Holy Spirit leads us down to walk around the white linen curtained enclosure, which surrounds the Tabernacle in the Wilderness. Here you will want to examine closely the picture of the Tabernacle in the front of this book.

As we approach the outer court we see some sixty pillars of acacia wood. Those pillars, standing some eight feet nine inches in height, are connected by bars of silver from which are hung the fine-twined linen curtains. One cannot see over or under these curtains.

As we walk around we come to the east entrance of the outer court. Here, at the gate of the court, which is the *only* entrance, we find a beautiful three-colored linen curtain. As a man stands before the white curtain, immediately he is face to face with the fact that he is a sinner, and he cannot enter as he is. God demands holiness. God has a standard of righteousness from which sinful man falls short. Here, the Holy Spirit begins to reveal to man his burden of sin and the desperate wickedness of his heart, which shuts him out from communion with a holy God. Shuts him out? *Oh, no!* There *is* a way— a *God-provided way!* Man may enter by the *one* gate and come to the Brazen Altar where the sacrifice is burning continually—the lamb whose blood was shed indicating a counterpart of the sacrifice of Christ Who shed His blood paying our penalty for sin.

THE ONE WAY OF APPROACH

Though man is a sinner, doomed to die for his sins ("The wages of sin is death") yet there is the innocent lamb, shedding his blood as a sacrifice, which is typical of Christ, the Lamb of God, going to the Cross and shedding His blood in our place. Thus the man who believes—who, at the Brazen Altar, believes and accepts—is forgiven. His weight of sin is lifted, remembered no more against him forever. In newness of life he may go on to the Laver for cleansing and on to the Mercy Seat where God will meet him in sweet fellowship.

The Book of Romans unfolds the way by which sinful man may approach a holy God. We can consider only a few points briefly, but you should read the Book of Romans carefully with this in view. It shows us clearly first of all, that natural man is without hope, without Christ, without God, a sinner before God. Paul begins in chapter 1:18 to point out that the scarlet sinner, the deeply-dyed sinner, the drunkard, the harlot, the murderer, the adulterer is lost; God has given them up to their vile affections. And anyone reading those verses would immediately agree that man is in need of salvation, and in order to be redeemed he needs to be clothed upon with God's perfect robe of righteousness.

Standing there before those white, fine-twined linen curtains we say, "Oh, Holy Spirit, how can man, devoid of God's standard of righteousness, lost, undone, how can he ever enter in and meet Thee at the blood-sprinkled Mercy Seat?" Yes, for the natural man that's the problem! I know there are many who endeavor to have fellowship with the eternal God, who talk about God, the Great Loving Spirit. But they have never, never come by God's way of approach as outlined in His Book and as is so clearly taught in the Tabernacle in the Wilderness. I realize my responsibility in making this teaching as plain as possible, with the Holy Spirit's empowering, for I am speaking to you who have eternal souls to be saved or lost. Let me warn you— unless you come in God's way, by Christ Jesus, the *only* way of approach, you will spend all eternity in separation from Him, an ever-living soul in everlasting darkness! But that's not God's will, and He has provided for you a way of escape.

CHAPTER III

The Brazen Altar

NOW OPEN YOUR BIBLES TO EXODUS 27 AND, AS YOU
read and consult the picture in the front of this
book, we shall study together the Brazen Altar.

We have already considered the general over-
all picture of the Tabernacle in the Wilderness:
its outer court, curtained off by curtains of pure,
white fine-twined linen, and its one gate of entrance
with a curtain of blue, purple and scarlet.

SALVATION FROM SIN

Now we consider the first article of furniture
in the Tabernacle, placed inside and near the one
gate of entrance, namely, the Brazen Altar. Coming
to the Brazen Altar is the first step a sinful man
must take on his way to the Holy of Holies, where
he can stand before God pardoned, cleansed, and
able to have fellowship with Him. Now, come with
me to the one gate, and let us push back the blue,

32

purple, and scarlet curtain and enter in. There before us stands the Brazen Altar, and on the hot coals lies the sacrificial lamb which has been slain and its blood sprinkled above the Mercy Seat. This is typical of Christ who shed His blood and gave His life that we might be forgiven. Sacrifice is God-ordained. When Adam and Eve sinned and were driven out of the Garden of Eden, God gave them coats of skin. Innocent animals had to give up their lives in order to obtain those coats.

Cain and Abel, sons of Adam and Eve, both had heard the way of approach—the way a sinful man could come to a Holy God. Abel believed God's Word; he came to the altar with a substitute, a spotless lamb. The lamb was slain, the blood applied, and an offering was made as God ordained. God had respect unto Abel's offering because it was a blood sacrifice. Fire came down and consumed the offering. Cain also had heard of God's way of approach. But he preferred to come in his own way, so he brought the fruits of his own labor. God did not have respect unto his offering and did not testify to it by consuming fire.

After the flood Noah built an altar before he built a house. Abram in Genesis 12 built an altar before he pitched the tent. Are you putting God first in your life? Have you come to the Brazen Altar —the Cross of Christ—God's one and only way of reconciliation? You may be highly successful in business, with good health, a lovely family, everything favorable from a worldly standpoint, but if you have not come to the Cross of Christ for forgiveness you are dead and spiritually separated from God. If you come to the moment of death not reconciled to God and die in your sins, you will be forever separated from Him. It is an awful thing to contemplate.

What do we learn from the Brazen Altar as we approach it? God's Word says that without the shedding of blood there is no remission of sin, and upon this Brazen Altar, back in the Old Testament days sacrifices were consumed by fire. This teaches us that sin is punishable by death. The soul that sinneth shall surely die. It also teaches us that an innocent substitute must die in the sinner's place. The slain lamb, the goat, the bullock were Israel's substitutes that shed their blood typical of Christ's atoning death on the Cross. So in the New Testament we find these words, "Behold the Lamb of God which taketh away the sin of the world." Jesus Christ, God's sacrificial lamb, died for your sins, for mine—died in your place, in my place. If you would go home to be with the Lord, you must needs go by the way of the Cross.

SALVATION BY GRACE ALONE

Now the Altar itself, standing in front of the one gate of entrance, was five cubits square. If you

34

know anything about numbers in the Bible, you know that five is the number of grace, six is the number of man, seven is the number of perfection, eight is the new beginning, and so on. The number five runs throughout the Tabernacle in the Wilderness, indicating that by grace we are saved.

Note that the Altar was made of wood overlaid with brass. Wood speaks of the humanity of the Lord Jesus, God manifest in the flesh. Brass is capable of enduring the fire. Jesus on the Cross was tested by the fires of God's wrath, and in that He revealed His perfection and sinlessness. Second, the Brazen Altar stood upon the desert sands, not upon some high exalted place. It could be approached without effort. Get it! No steps to the Brazen Altar! No stepping stones to Christ, no works of merit are required in order to have reconciliation. Come sinner, just as you are!

I recall a sad sight which I saw in an eastern city. An old woman on her knees was painfully toiling up a flight of about 350 stone steps. At each step she paused, saying a prayer. She did not know that salvation is a free gift of God if we come by Jesus Christ, God's way of approach unto Himself. Oh, if all could know and if all would heed the outstretched arms and the gentle voice saying, "Come unto me."

SALVATION FOR ALL

At the four corners of the Altar were horns, and the horn in Scripture denotes power and strength.

It says, "Bind the sacrifice with cords, with the horns of the altar, and so the burnt offering sacrifice was bound to the altar." My Lord on the morning of Calvary was nailed to the Cross. Hands and feet were pierced and He was bound to the Cross as the sacrifice in Old Testament times was bound to the Brazen Altar. The horns pointed to the four corners of the earth. I've said it once, and I repeat that whosoever will may come out of every tribe, kindred, tongue, and nation! Jesus will have His witnesses from all the earth before He comes again.

Then do you know about the ashes of the burnt sacrifice? When the sacrifice was completely consumed, the ashes were carefully removed, carried in a covered pan to a clean place outside the camp (Exodus 27:1-9). This proved that the fire of God's wrath was carried away. Joseph of Arimathaea begged that dear body—wrapped it in clean linen cloth and placed it in a new tomb where no corrupting flesh had ever lain. Then, showing His complete satisfaction, God raised Jesus from the dead. This is the Gospel, the Gospel of grace, the Gospel which is the power of God unto salvation, and will you hear me, Christians? That is our main job, to get this Gospel out, to tell abroad the good news that Christ died for the sins of men, that He was buried, that He rose again the third day according to the Scriptures. Why be taken up with anything else?

We are to warn men to repent and believe the Gospel or perish!

THE ONE WAY OF SALVATION

And now in closing, I want you to read a few verses from Hebrews 9 beginning at verse 11. See how clearly this refers to the Old Testament sacrifice. "But Christ being come an high priest of good things to come, by a greater and more perfect tabernacle, not made with hands, that is to say, not of this building; Neither by the blood of goats and calves, but by his own blood he entered in once into the holy place, having obtained eternal redemption for us. For if the blood of bulls and of goats, and the ashes of an heifer sprinkling the unclean, sanctifieth to the purifying of the flesh: how much more shall the blood of Christ, who through the eternal spirit offered Himself without spot to God, [there you have the Trinity] purge your conscience from dead works to serve the living God?"

Hebrews 9:26: "For then must he often have suffered since the foundation of the world: but now once in the end of the world hath he appeared to put away sin by the sacrifice of himself." He'll take your sins and put them behind his back never to remember them against you forever! How complete is the deliverance our God has provided for sinful man!

Friends of mine, outside of Christ, with no

peace in your heart, will you come God's way? There are many sandy foundations that will not abide the storm of God's wrath in the days ahead. Only those upon the rock Christ Jesus will be free from the judgment to come. Christ died for your sins. Now He is saying to you that He is not willing that you should perish. Why not make this great decision to-day and receive Christ as your personal Saviour. Out in the great radio audience, scattered across the nations of earth,—you may be hidden away in some lonely place—some desolate place—maybe on a sick bed—maybe behind prison bars—wherever you are, you can look up into the Father's face and say, "God be merciful to me a sinner." And you can be assured that He hears you. Jesus says, "Him that cometh unto me I will in no wise cast out." He will hear your prayer, He will save your soul if you will only let Him.

CHAPTER IV

The Laver

TODAY WE SHALL STUDY THE LAVER, THE SECOND
article of furniture found in the outer court in the
Tabernacle in the Wilderness. It is at the Laver that
man is cleansed, after passing the Brazen Altar.
"Who shall ascend into the hill of the Lord, or who
shall stand in His holy place?" He that hath clean
hands says the Psalmist.

Let us note what God's Word tells us in Exodus
30 verses 18–21: "Thou shalt make a laver of brass,
and his foot also of brass, to wash withal: and thou
shalt put it between the tabernacle of the congregation and the altar, and thou shalt put water therein.
For Aaron and his sons shall wash their hands and
their feet . . . when they go into the tabernacle of
the congregation, they shall wash with water, that
they die not. . . ."

THE SECOND STEP TO FELLOWSHIP

Near the door of entrance to the Tabernacle stood the Brazen Altar upon which a sacrifice burned continually, teaching the eternal truth that without the shedding of blood there is no remission, or forgiveness, of sin. There is no way, under heaven, my dear friend, for you to be forgiven of your sins apart from the shedding of the blood of the Lamb of God which takes away the sin of the world. Thus the Brazen Altar in the Tabernacle points to Calvary—to Christ's sacrifice for our sins. Here at the Brazen Altar man is reconciled to God through the death of an innocent substitute who dies in his place. But now, as a man redeemed and forgiven, proceeds toward the Holy of Holies he comes from the Brazen Altar to the Laver for cleansing, to be purified, made holy, for "Without holiness no man shall see the Lord." As Aaron, the High Priest, and his sons left the Brazen Altar, moving on toward the Tabernacle proper, they must stop at the Laver, there to wash their hands and feet and be cleansed by the water.

Beloved fellow pilgrim, right here is a most important lesson. You deserved death, but Christ died in your place, paying your penalty for sin. You believe this, and therefore you are forgiven and are at peace with God. Your past sins are blotted out. You are saved by Christ's wonderful atoning blood.

But wait, you long to have communion and fellowship with God, to come close to your heavenly
Father as a child loves to come to a beloved earthly
father. But God is in the Holy of Holies, above the
blood-sprinkled Mercy Seat and inaccessable to you.
To have fellowship with Him you must have clean
hands and feet—cleansed from daily defilement.
Well, here the Laver is God's wonderful provision
for cleansing! Remember the Laver stands between
the Brazen Altar and the door of the Tabernacle.
It is the second step in the way as man approaches
God in order to have sweet fellowship with Him.

CLEANSED BY GOD'S WORD

In Exodus 30 verse 18: "Thou shalt make a
Laver of brass." There are no dimensions given such
as we find concerning the Brazen Altar and other
articles of furniture—no dimensions because the
Laver is a type of the Word of God. There are no
dimensions or limitations to the Word of God. We
are told the Laver was made of brass. According to
Exodus 38:8 it was made of the brass of the looking
glasses, given freely by the women of Israel to be
melted and made into the Laver. Looking glasses
in the days of Moses were rare and were made of
polished brass. These mirrors were prized posses-
sions of the women of Israel, and doubtless they
spent a good deal of time looking into them.

Now as you come to the Word of God—your

looking glass—and as you read and meditate, with an obedient heart, God shows you the things in your life which are not pleasing unto Him. Thereby you see your need of daily washing. You confess your sin and turn away from it, and you are washed. As the priests of old approached the polished brass of the Laver, they saw that in themselves dwelt no good thing. The burnished Laver revealed any defilements that they had contacted in their daily walk, and they washed. This indicated to them also the need for inner cleansing.

The inspired Word of God from Genesis to Revelation is our Laver to which we should come daily for cleansing, reading, and looking into the mirror of God's Word. The Brazen Altar, where the slain lamb is sacrificed, takes care of the sin question. All past sins are forgiven, blotted out. But the Laver is for *daily* cleansing, and you need to be cleansed if you are to have fellowship with a Holy God.

In Exodus 38:20 Aaron and his sons are told to wash lest they die. Unless we wash, we die. To what? We die to fellowship with God. True, those who stay at the Brazen Altar (the cross) will be saved as though by fire. But they are not cleansed from the defilement of this sinful world about them, and they know nothing of the sweetness of fellowship with God, when He reveals or makes Himself real to His child.

THE EXAMPLE OF PETER

Now will you take your Bibles and turn to John 13. This is a wonderful, rich chapter. My soul has been blessed again and again as I have read and meditated upon it. At the Last Supper, the Feast of the Passover, Jesus knew that His hour was come, that He would soon depart out of this world unto the Father. He had His beloved disciples there with Him in that upper room. They had partaken of the pascal lamb. Christ, the true Pascal Lamb, was at the table with them. Supper being ended, Jesus, the second person of the Trinity, knowing that the Father had given all things into His hands, knowing that He was come from God and would return to Him, arose from the supper. He laid aside His outer garments and took a towel and girded Himself. Think of it—the Creator of all things, the One who literally holds together the great universe, the stars, and the planets, became as a servant, and what did He do? He poured water into a basin and began to wash the disciples' feet and to wipe them with a towel wherewith He was girded. Do you see it? He was fulfilling the type of the Laver—cleansing. "Then cometh he to Simon Peter: and Peter said unto Him, Lord, dost thou wash my feet. Jesus answered and said unto Him, what I do thou knowest not now but thou shalt know hereafter." But Peter said unto Him, "Thou shalt never wash my

THE TABERNACLE IN THE WILDERNESS

feet." (John 13:6–10) And notice how tenderly Jesus replied, "If I wash thee not, thou hast no part with me."

Now consider this, my friend: Peter was a disciple—forgiven, saved, and for him the sin question was settled. But what about the daily walk? Regarding being washed from daily defilement, Jesus said to Peter, "If I wash thee not, thou hast no part with me"—in fellowship. Right there between the Brazen Altar and the Laver is the place where many a believer stops in Christian growth, for he does not wish to be cleansed from worldly defilement to lead a clean and separated life. If such is your case, my brother, do you wonder why you have little power, why your testimony is weak, why your prayers are not answered, why you do not enjoy fellowship with our Lord? It is that you are not coming for cleansing and turning away from your sins. Peter realized this when, looking to Jesus he said, "Lord, not my feet only but also my hands and my head." And, "Jesus said to him, he that is washed needeth not save to wash his feet but is clean everywhit." Yes, my friend, at the Brazen Altar you are forgiven, but we all need to be washed at the Laver with the water of God's word.

There are thousands out in the radio audience, and some here no doubt, who need to come to the Brazen Altar and accept Christ as their personal Saviour, realizing that Christ bore their sins in His own body. But I believe there are millions who, having come to the Brazen Altar, are saved, forgiven, but they need to go on to the Laver, to be cleansed. May God open the eyes of your understanding to see the wonder of His blessings which He showers upon those who will go "deeper yet"— who come close to their Lord in sweetness of fellowship. God calls us to a separated life. In Ephesians 5:26 we are told, "That He might sanctify and cleanse with the washing of water by the word."

Oh, do not stay at the cross, but go on to the Laver beyond the door of the Tabernacle, unto the Table of Shewbread, walking in the light as He is in the light—on to fellowship. I am sure you are not satisfied just to be saved as though by fire with no reward, no fruit, no fellowship with Him! May God open your eyes to see the wonders of His blessings to those who come close to their Lord in sweetness of fellowship—empowered, prayers answered, appropriating His peace and His rest. Oh, my friend, come and experience all these good things God has provided for His children. Oh! I tell you it is wonderful! I have found this communion with my Lord so sweet that I have had to ask God to turn off the Glory, I could stand no more! Do come, my friend! God is faithful.

CHAPTER V

The Table of Shewbread

Turn in your Bibles, please, to Leviticus, chapter 24, beginning at the fifth verse. Pray with me today that many will find Jesus, the Bread of Life, and be sustained in this pilgrimage journey.

FURNITURE ARRANGED LIKE A CROSS

There were in the Tabernacle in the Wilderness six articles of furniture. In the outer court, there were the Brazen Altar and the Laver; in the Tabernacle proper (the Holy Place) there were the Table of Shewbread, the Golden Candlestick, and the Altar of Incense; and in the Holy of Holies there was the Ark of the Covenant, covered by the blood-sprinkled Mercy Seat. Now with your chart before you, please notice that these articles of furniture are placed in the form of a cross. The centerpiece of the cross is seen in the straight line extending from the

46

Brazen Altar through the Laver and Altar of Incense to the Ark of the Covenant. The two arms of the cross are the Golden Candlestick and the Table of Shewbread. Jesus said, "I am the bread of life . . . I am the light of the world. . . ." (John 6:35; 8:12), and we may think of the bread and light needed by a spiritually hungry and darkened world as extending outward from the two arms of this cross.

THE PLACE OF FELLOWSHIP

Today, let us consider briefly the Table of Shewbread. It is also called the Table of the "bread of faces," a figure of speech representing the presence of the Lord. Hence, the bread on this Table is also designated the "present bread" or the "presence bread." Let us notice the way, according to the plan of the Tabernacle, that a sinful man *must* come if he is to have fellowship with the holy God. Let me drive home to you the fact that man *must* come God's way; all other ways are useless. First of all, he must come to the Cross of Christ, represented by the Brazen Altar. Here, repentant man is reconciled to God on the basis of the death and shed blood of Christ, the innocent substitute Who died in his place. Then, after he has been justified by faith in Christ Who bore His sins, he must allow the sins that crop up in his life from day to day to be cleansed away by the Word of God. This cleansing by the water of the the Word is represented by the Laver, where the priests had to cleanse their hands and feet daily before they could enter the Holy Place and partake of the bread of presence. So, likewise, we who have had our sins forgiven at the Cross must confess our sins, as they are exposed by the Word of God, so that we may maintain continuous fellowship with the holy God.

How well I remember when a young lad on an orange ranch, that around noontime Mother would call me in from work or play and say, "Charlie, dinner is ready, so come on in after you have washed your hands and face." Well, one day I was really hungry, so I just gave my hands and face a quick rinse. Then I went in and sat down at the table, even though I knew I had not done a thorough job. But though I was a member of the family, though I was born into that family, Mother's sharp eye saw my unclean condition, and she would not let me have fellowship at that table. She took me by the ear and marched me out to the wash basin and saw to it that my hands and face were really polished. Then, and not until then, was I permitted to fellowship at the table where I could eat that good home-cooked food—that old-fashioned home-made bread that only Mother could make. I'd like to have a loaf right now!

Now the Table of Shewbread speaks of fellowship with God, just as a dinner table suggests fellowship with our friends. When we desire to know a friend a little more intimately, when we desire to discuss matters of mutual concern and interest, the thing we naturally do is to invite that friend to dinner—to break bread with us. So, with this Table of Shewbread, God takes the things with which we are familiar to teach us spiritual things. God and His Son Jesus Christ long to have fellowship with their blood-bought, redeemed children. And we who are privileged to be children of God through faith in Christ should have as our chief desire that of coming to an increasingly more intimate fellowship with God and Christ. David said, "As the hart panteth after the water brooks, so pants my soul after thee, O God" (Psalm 42:1). And Paul, though he had experienced glorious success in preaching the Gospel, said, as he sat in a dark Roman prison, that he counted all things but loss in comparison with the glory of having fellowship with Christ (Philippians 3:9, 10). God has provided the means whereby we may satisfy this desire of ours to know Him better. As Israel in the Old Testament days, through the God-appointed priests, had fellowship with God at the Table of Shewbread, so in New Testament times, we who are true children of God can have fellowship with God through His Word, the written Bread of Life, and through Christ, the Living Bread of Life. Christ said, ". . . I am the bread of life . . . the words that I speak unto you,

49

they are spirit, and they are life" (John 6:35, 63).
And Peter, seeking the fellowship of God, said to
Christ, ". . . To whom shall we go? Thou hast the
words of eternal life" (John 6:68).

THE SHEWBREAD

Now in Leviticus 24:5–10, we read the instructions concerning the way the loaves of shewbread
were made. According to verse 5, fine flour had to be
taken. That means that wheat had to be harvested,
then separated from the chaff at the threshing floor,
and finally ground at the mill before it could be the
fine flour required for the shewbread. So our Lord
Jesus Christ, the God-appointed wheat, was cut
down, sifted by suffering, ground and bruised fine
in the mill of God's judgment against sin so that he
might become the bread of God's presence, the
shewbread, pure and holy before God and man.
Fine flour means no unevenness, no lumps, no
coarseness, and so it suggests the sinlessness of
Christ. Even His enemies testified of His sinlessness.
Pilate said, ". . . I find no fault in this man"
(Luke 23:4). Pilate's wife said, ". . . Have nothing to do with that just man . . ." (Matthew 27:19).
Judas Iscariot said, ". . . I have sinned in that I
have betrayed innocent blood" (Matthew 27:4).
The centurion said, ". . . Surely this was a right-
eous man" (Luke 23:47).

CONDITIONS FOR FELLOWSHIP

Continuing on with verse 5 and into verse 6 we read, ". . . bake twelve cakes thereof: two-tenth deals shall be in one cake. And thou shalt set them in two rows, six on a row." Each of these twelve cakes represented a tribe of the children of Israel. The same amount of flour was used in each cake, and they were arranged in an orderly, symmetrical pattern on the Table. As represented on the Table, no tribe could think of itself as superior or separate from the other tribes. This brings home to us the powerful truth that we cannot hope to have fellowship with a holy God unless we have our hearts cleansed from all bitterness, pride, and enmity against a Christian brother. To have fellowship and communion with God, we must be one with the family of God.

But reading on in verse 6, we discern another condition that must be met if we are to have fellowship with God. These loaves are to be set upon the *pure* Table before the Lord. How incongruous for any one who was impure to come to such a Table and expect to have fellowship with the holy God!

Now, keeping these facts in mind, turn to I Corinthians, where we see a specific New Testament application of these truths pictured in the Table of Shewbroad. According to I Corinthians 6:11, the church at Corinth was composed of members who had been washed, sanctified, and justified in Christ. However, dissensions and strife had arisen because these people began to look more to their human leaders than to Christ. Along with these dissensions, sins of the flesh, such as fornication, had been permitted amongst the members without any steps being taken by the Church to discipline the offenders.

Therefore, Paul stresses the necessity for believers to understand that they are one with one another. He says in I Corinthians 10:16, "The cup of blessing which we bless, is it not the communion of the blood of Christ? . . . *For we being many are one bread and one body:* for we are all partakers of that one bread." One loaf—Oh Brother, listen to me, *listen to me:* in God's sight there's but one body, one loaf, and that loaf has been brought together by tribulation, by being ground fine, by the suffering through which each believer must go. Thus I say it on God's authority that denominations (much as I respect them) are secondary in God's sight. And since we who are blood-bought, redeemed children of God are one in Christ, we are to have a communion with God at the Table of Shewbread which is free from all enmity and bitterness toward those who are likewise fellow-heirs with Christ. When you come by the Brazen Altar, by the Laver, to the Table of Shewbread, there to be in God's presence, do you come with an unforgiving spirit? Do you come with bitterness in your heart——with hatred, jealousy, with sins of the flesh? First, cleanse your heart of all these things; have love in your heart toward your brother, and then you will be ready for fellowship at God's Table. This is where so many Christians fail—and it is so very important!

Again, Paul says to the Corinthians, "For as often as ye eat this bread, and drink this cup, ye do shew the Lord's death till he come. Wherefore whosoever shall eat this bread, and drink this cup of the Lord unworthily, . . . eateth and drinketh condemnation to himself, not discerning the Lord's body" (I Corinthians 11:26–29). Thus, let everyone examine himself before partaking of communion, and let the Lord point out all the things that are displeasing to Him. Then, if we confess our sins, we know God is faithful and just to forgive us our sins and to cleanse us from all unrighteousness (I John 1:9). Thus, ". . . If we walk in the light, as he is in the light, we have fellowship one with another, and the blood of Jesus Christ his Son cleanseth us from all sin" (I John 1:7).

Where are you, my friend? Are you still at the Cross, saved as though by fire? Let's leave the first principles of repentance and go beyond the Laver into the Holy Place, and there sit at the Table in fellowship with Him, feasting upon Him, and at rest with Him. How we do need His fellowship and His rest—as we travel on this wilderness journey.

We can have it if we will press on, beyond the Brazen Altar. Will you do that today, fellow believer?

CHAPTER VI

The Golden Candlestick of the Tabernacle

THE TABERNACLE IS AN OLD TESTAMENT PRE-PIC-
ture of the redemptive work of the Lord Jesus
Christ. In 1445 B.C., the Lord gave Moses instructions on how to build the Tabernacle where He
might dwell among His people. Moses carried out
these instructions very carefully, and when the
Tabernacle was set up, Exodus 40:34 records that
the glory of the Lord filled it. Then, fifteen hundred
years later, the Apostle John says concerning Christ:
"The Word was made flesh and dwelt [*lit.* taber-
nacled] among us (and we beheld his glory, the
glory as of the only begotten of the Father,) full of
grace and truth." (John 1:14)

Hence, Jesus Christ is the fulfillment of that
pre-picture of Himself represented by the Tabernacle in the Wilderness. Continuing on into the
Gospel of John we read of Christ, the Lamb of

God Who taketh away the sins of the world (John 1:29), and this calls to our minds the Brazen Altar of the Tabernacle where the sacrificial lamb was slain. In John 6:35, Christ declares Himself to be the Bread of Life, and this answers to the Table of Shewbread. Then in John 8:12, the Lord says, ". . . I am the light of the world, . . ." and we remember the Golden Candlestick.

The Golden Candlestick, then, points to Christ as the light of the world. How desperately the natural man needs spiritual light! He enters this world blinded to the things of God, for according to II Corinthians 4:4, Satan has blinded his mind lest the light of Christ should shine upon him. Being thus blinded, the natural man refuses to receive the spiritual truths revealed in the Bible. Every man outside of Christ is therefore in desperate need of spiritual light, for only through the light of Christ as He shines through God's Word can he perceive his lost condition, his need for the forgiveness of sins, reconciliation, and cleansing. Only through God's Word can he find light for his pathway, so that he can be delivered from the awful problems that beset his life.

That is your need, my friend outside of Christ. The entrance of God's Word giveth light. You who are listening across the nations of earth, hear me! You who today are blinded to the wonders of God's love, mercy, and grace, listen to me: The God of love is not willing that you should perish, for He has provided a way of escape. And when you come in God's way in simple, believing faith, your sin-darkened soul is illuminated as you embrace Christ, the Light of Life. Thus we beseech you today to come to the true Light, and then live the rest of your life in accordance with God's Word, the entrance of which giveth light.

But now I want you to notice some details of the Golden Candlestick and the truths which they serve to bring forth.

MADE OF BEATEN, PURE GOLD

In Exodus 25:31 we read: "And thou shalt make a candlestick of pure gold: of beaten work shall the candlestick be made. . . ." The gold of this Candlestick had to go through two processes of refining: it had to be burned in white heat to be made *pure,* and then it had to be carefully *beaten* by skillful craftsmen until it was formed into a beautiful, symmetrical candlestick. It would be well for you to underline the words "pure" and "beaten" in your Bibles, for they point to the sufferings which Christ, the pure and spotless One, had to endure so that He might shine forth as the Light of the World.

Consider the sufferings Christ endured. He knew poverty. After boyhood He was homeless, for He confessed that whereas the foxes had holes and the birds of the air had nests, He had not where to lay His head. He was despised, misjudged, and falsely accused. As He walked the dusty roads to Palestine, He knew hunger, thirst, and weariness. But the climax of His sufferings came at Gethsemane and Calvary, where he felt not only the sting of the lash, the shame of the spittle, the crown of thorns, and the awful pain of the nails and the Cross, but worse than any of these—the awfulness of being forsaken by God and experiencing God's wrath for the world's sin.

My Lord was pure, harmless, sinless, perfect before God. But it pleased God to bruise Him, so that my precious Lord was also beaten and fashioned to become fitted as the captain of my salvation. This Jesus, the Light of the World, God's Golden Candlestick, was made perfect through suffering that He might give forth light to His people as they make their pilgrimage journey through this world so full of suffering and heartache.

ALL OF ONE PIECE

Continuing on in Exodus 25:31, 32 we read that the six branches of this Golden Candlestick were to be of one piece (three on a side) with the central shaft of the Candlestick. Both the central shaft and its branches were beaten into shape from one lump of gold.

Now in John, chapter 15, Christ pictured Himself as the vine and His Church as the branches. Just as the branches of the vine are one with the vine it-self, so also the branches of the Golden Candlestick were one with its central shaft, and thus we may think of the branches of the Golden Candlestick as representing God's people who are joined to Christ by faith.

But when we are joined by faith to the Lord, we are a long way from being like Him. So, at the moment of conversion, God begins the process of conforming us to the image of Christ. How is this process carried on? Remember that the Candlestick was fashioned by beating one lump of gold into the central shaft and the branches. The same process used to fashion the central shaft was used to fashion the branches. In like manner, we become conformed to the likeness of Christ by partaking of the suffer-ings of Christ. Thus Paul desired the fellowship of Christ's sufferings so that he might be conformed to His image (Phillipians 3:10). As God permits suf-ferings to come into our lives, we are conformed to the image of Christ. By suffering, by tribulation, by persecution, by trials that come to us through God's permissive will, we are progressively "beaten" into shape so that eventually we might be conformed to Christ's image.

Thus, my friend, if you are yielded to God, every trial that comes your way can be a gracious blow, conforming you to the image of Christ. Paul spoke of our light affliction which worketh for us a far more exceeding and eternal weight of glory. (II Corinthians 4:17). And beloved, listen, as I look back over thirty-seven years of Gospel preaching I can say that God has permitted many hammer blows in my life. There were blows of many kinds: heavy financial losses, serious illnesses in my family, unfair accusations; and it was not easy to take them. But when I look back and see it all in the light of eternity and realize that this is the day of my suffering, the trial of my faith, I can rejoice! For I am a part of the Candlestick, a branch that is being fashioned by God's workmanship to be made like Christ. I am His forever, and He is mine. Hallelujah! Oh, let us not think it strange when fiery trials come our way. These are the trials of our faith. This is the day of our fellowship in His suffering, and God's loving hand is fashioning us as beaten gold in order that we might be conformed to the image of His Son.

I have learned something, and I pass it on to you, young converts. As you yield to God under testings and trials, you will be brought closer to Him! You will come to know Him better and love Him more, as you find Him faithful in every trial. And your light will shine for Him the brighter! I've seen people in the hour of deepest trials, passing through waters of great sorrow, yet their faces simply shone with the reflected glory of Christ. Oh, as you rest in His goodness, as you read His Word and plead the promises, your faith grows and you can rejoice in sorrow. The old nature is beaten away as you yield, and the light of the indwelling Holy Spirit shines out as He takes the things of Christ and reveals them to you.

WICKS CONSTANTLY TRIMMED

Now consider the fact that the Candlestick provided the only source of light for the Tabernacle. It was very important that the wicks be trimmed so that the light would not grow dim. Thus, it was the daily task of the priest to go into the Tabernacle with a tweezer and a little golden pan. With the tweezer he would lift the partly burned wicks and break off the black carbon, so that the light could shine more brightly. The pieces of carbon were placed in the golden pan and taken away. So as we daily come to the light of the Word, Christ our High Priest draws us a little closer to Himself; He cleanses us and takes away the things that are not of the Spirit, that our light may shine more brightly.

Is your light a little bit dim? Is the flesh keeping the Holy Spirit from shining forth in true brightness from your life? Let Christ draw you a little closer to Himself. Let Him remove the things that are hindering your testimony. These are dark days, and this old world needs light.

And friend of mine, if you need light, look unto Jesus Who is the Light of the World, entrust yourself to Him, follow Him that you might have the light of life. He has promised to receive all who come to Him in faith believing.

CHAPTER VII

The Golden Altar of Incense

KEEP YOUR BIBLE OPEN, PLEASE, TO EXODUS 30:1–10, that passage recording the commands God gave to Moses for the construction of the Golden Altar. Today we study the third and last item of furniture in the Holy Place. We have seen how the other two pieces of furniture in the Holy Place pointed to Christ and to the position the believer occupies by virtue of his relationship to Christ. We saw how the Table of Shewbread pointed to Christ the Bread of Life, and we saw how the Golden Candlestick typified Christ, the Light of the World. But we also saw that the Table of Shewbread showed how individual believers are to live in harmony and fellowship with each other as they have fellowship with Christ and the Father; likewise, the Golden Candlestick taught that believers are to be lights in the world as they are joined to Christ.

As we read concerning the Golden Altar of Incense in Exodus 30, we ask ourselves, "In what way does this object of furniture point to Christ and the relationship that believers bear to Him?" In dealing with the typical teaching of the Tabernacle (as with all typical teaching), we must be very careful not to allow our foolish imaginations to run riot. The interpretation we give to these various parts of the Tabernacle must be based upon God's Word—not upon our own ideas. In the last analysis, God's Word itself is its own best commentary, and so let us turn to it now to find the meaning of the Golden Altar of Incense.

THE BIBLICAL MEANING OF THE GOLDEN ALTAR

In Revelation 8:3, 4 we read: "And another angel came and stood at the altar, having a golden censer, and there was given unto him much incense, that he should offer it with the prayers of all saints upon the golden altar which was before the throne. And the smoke of the incense, which came with the prayers of the saints, ascended up before God out of the angel's hand." Here we find incense connected with prayer. Now let us also turn to Luke 1:9, 10, where we find another reference to the fact that prayer accompanied the offering up of incense: "According to the custom of the priest's office, his lot was to burn incense when he [i.e., Zacharias] went into the temple of the Lord. And the whole multitude of the people were praying without at the time of incense." Therefore, it is safe to say that the Golden Altar of Incense points to Christ's intercessory prayers and the prayers which believers are able to pray by virtue of their relationship to Him. First of all, then, let us consider how this Golden Altar typifies the intercessory work of Christ, and then how it points to the prayers of the saints.

CHRIST'S INTERCESSORY WORK FOR US

In the Tabernacle in the Wilderness there were two altars, the Brazen Altar and this Golden Altar of Incense. On the Brazen Altar a sacrifice was constantly being offered up, whereas God made it explicit to Moses that no offering or sacrifice was to be placed on the Golden Altar. The reason for this is quite apparent, for we have already seen that while the Brazen Altar typified the atoning death and finished work of Christ upon the Cross, the Golden Altar pointed to Christ's work of intercessory prayer. The first Altar pointed to Christ's suffering and death—to the atoning work which He did while still upon this earth. It was made of brass; it had no crown, and it thus bespeaks the suffering and humiliation of our precious Lord. But the second Altar, the Altar of Incense, was made of gold, and its top was a crown of gold extending outward from each corner in the form of a horn, and thus it points to Christ's glory and exaltation—to His work of intercession which He is now doing as our ascended Lord Who is far above all principalities and powers.

Hebrews 1:3 says concerning Christ that ". . . when he had by himself purged our sins, sat down on the right hand of the Majesty on high." Christ's first work was to purge our sins, and this was foreshadowed by the Brazen Altar. But now Christ is engaged in His second work for us. Hebrews 7:25 says that, ". . . he ever liveth to make intercession for us." And this work was foreshadowed by the Golden Altar.

What a wonderful thing it is to know that our Lord is constantly interceding for us! Whatever our needs may be, known or unknown to us, Christ prays to the Father that we may have them supplied. He ever liveth to make intercession for us! He that keepeth Israel never slumbers or sleeps!

But wait a minute, friend of mine. You can never benefit from Christ's work, typified by the Golden Altar, until you accept what He has done for you at the Brazen Altar. You can never have the confidence that Christ intercedes on your behalf, until you have accepted His atoning death for your sins. Remember, to get to the Golden Altar you must first pass by the Brazen Altar where the sacrificial lamb was slain and offered up. So likewise, to know Christ's constant watch-care over your life, you must first humbly kneel at the foot of the Cross, con-

fess your sins, and trust in Christ and the finished
work of paying the penalty for your sins which He
accomplished for you there.

CHRIST'S INTERCESSORY WORK IN US

The fact that Christ lives to make intercession
for us constantly does not mean, however, that we
should not engage in prayer ourselves. Rather, the
Word commands that we should "pray without ceasing" (I Thessalonians 5:17), that we should pray
'. . . always with all prayer and supplication in the
Spirit, and watching thereunto with all persever-
ance and supplication for all saints" (Ephesians
6:18). While Christ is constantly praying for us
while seated at the right hand of the Father, we
should be continually engaged in prayer here upon
earth.

But you say, "Brother Fuller, how can I pray
without ceasing? How can I go on praying especially
when the affairs of life close in upon me?" My answer is that of course you cannot do this by yourself.
But God has provided a way in which the incense
of our prayers may constantly ascend to the throne
of grace. In Romans 8:26, 27 we read, "Likewise the
Spirit also helpeth our infirmities: for we know not
what we should pray for as we ought: but the Spirit
himself maketh intercession for us with groanings
which cannot be uttered. And he that searcheth the
hearts knoweth what is the mind of the Spirit, be-

cause he maketh intercession for the saints according to the will of God." This passage I have just read means that all who are born again have the Spirit of God abiding in them and interceding for them. The Holy Spirit is constantly interceding for us even when our attention is focused upon other things. At such times, we can sense His work by the groanings, by the inarticulate yearnings which are in our soul, and by the sense of Christ's presence which He constantly vouchsafes to us. Then, when we are finished with the affairs of the day, He may gently call us to the secret place of prayer, and there open our hearts to pray to the Father in the name of Christ. All true prayer must be initiated and inspired by the Holy Spirit, or else we will simply be praying as the Pharisee in the temple who prayed with himself.

Thus, it is our solemn responsibility as Christians so to walk in the Spirit, so to refrain from grieving or quenching the Spirit, that He will constantly have full sway in our hearts to carry on His work of intercession. But, friend of mine, let me repeat—You can never know what it is to have fellowship with God and Christ, you can never know the joys of answered prayer until you come first to the Brazen Altar (i.e., the Cross), the only place where you can find the forgiveness of sins and be born again. Then you must always wash at the Laver of the Word of God so that the incense of Spirit-inspired prayer may constantly ascend to God the Father in the name of Christ.

Now, let me point out some of the details of this Golden Altar which help to teach us the way we can be godly men and women whose fervent prayers avail much. First of all, incense of the Golden Altar was caused to rise by being set afire by a coal from the Brazen Altar. Since the Brazen Altar typifies the Cross of Christ, we learn from this that true prayer can come only from a heart which is inspired by a genuine love for the Cross of Christ. What does this mean? Paul said in Galatians 6:14: ". . . God forbid that I should glory save in the cross of our Lord Jesus Christ. . . ." Only when our chief delight, our chief glory, is in the Cross of Christ—only when we seek the glory and presence of God Himself rather than the praise of men, when like Paul we count all things but loss that we might know Christ —only then can our prayers be motivated by that love which will make them rise as incense to the throne of God. If your heart is filled with self-love, the love of money, pleasures, and gain, if your heart is filled with the cares of this world, you are not glorying in the Cross, and therefore there is no coal from off the Brazen Altar to cause the incense to ascend. Therefore, cleanse your hands, ye sinners, and purify your hearts, ye doubleminded, so that you might become righteous in heart and pray effectual, fervent prayers that avail much.

Again note that according to Exodus 30:7, 8, the incense was burned both in the morning and at evening, and at the very same time the wicks of the Golden Candlestick were trimmed. How beautiful! Just as the wicks in the Golden Candlestick burned brightest when the incense on the Golden Altar was set afire, so also our witness for Christ before a lost and dying world shines brightest when our hearts are aflame with Holy Spirit-inspired prayer.

A striking example of this truth is to be found in the call of Isaiah. In Isaiah 6:1–3 we read how Isaiah caught a vision of the glory of Christ (see John 12:41). Then, he confessed and repented of his self-love and sin, and the result was that a live coal was taken from the altar and his sin was forgiven. When the Lord said, "Whom shall I send, and who will go for us?" Isaiah answered, "Here am I; send me." Then God sent Isaiah forth to prophesy to Israel. For fifty years he shone as a light in the world, and today, though dead, he yet speaketh. Why? He prayed a prayer inspired by a love for the Cross of Christ, and in so doing, God trimmed his wick so that he became a burning and shining light for God and Christ in his generation.

Friend of mine, do you know the reality of Christ, of sins forgiven? Do you have the certain hope of eternal life? Kneel there by your radio today as this broadcast goes out to the nations of earth. Accept Christ as your personal Saviour—settle it today. And you, fellow believer, is your heart right with God so that you can pray in the Spirit and be a shining witness for Christ? Let God cleanse your life as He cleansed Isaiah's. Count all things but loss that you might know the excellency of the knowledge of Christ. Learn to pray the effectual, fervent prayer of the righteous man so that you may be a lighthouse in this sin-darkened world.

CHAPTER VIII

The Veil of the Tabernacle

AGAIN TAKE YOUR BIBLES AND TURN TO EXODUS 26:31: "And thou shalt make a veil of blue, and purple, and scarlet, and fine-twined linen of cunning work. . . ." There were three beautifully colored curtains in the Tabernacle in the Wilderness. The first one was at the gate of the entrance just before the Brazen Altar, the second was at the door of the Holy Place, and the third was the veil before the Ark of the Covenant in the Holy of Holies. Three curtains—one at the gate, one at the door, and one leading into the Holy of Holies.

A VEIL SEPARATES

Now, the meaning of the word "veil" is "to separate." Communion with the very presence of God was to be found only in the Holy of Holies, for God told Moses in Exodus 25:22 that He would meet and commune with him from above the blood-sprinkled

Mercy Seat. But notice how separated the Holy of Holies was from the surrounding encampment of the children of Israel. Three curtains had to be passed, each of which added to the sense of the great gulf which existed between God and man. Likewise, to enter the Holy of Holies, one had to pass the Brazen Altar, wash at the Laver, walk in the light of the Golden Candlestick, and come before the Altar of Incense before he was fit to come into the Holy of Holies and commune with Almighty God.

But remember this: while Aaron and his sons went twice each day to the Brazen Altar, the Laver, and then into the Holy Place to trim the lamps and place incense upon the Golden Altar, only once a year, on the Day of Atonement, did Aaron himself go beyond the veil of the Tabernacle and enter into the Holy of Holies. Read Hebrews 9:7, 8: "But into the second [i.e., the Holy of Holies] went the high priest alone once every year, not without blood, which he offered for himself and for the errors of the people. . . ."—the Holy Spirit thus signifying that the way into the holiest of all was not yet made manifest until the Veil of the Temple was rent when Christ died on Calvary. The Veil of the Tabernacle, then, emphasized the separation, the great gulf that existed between God and men until the Cross of Calvary.

Other usages of the word "veil" in the Bible carry with them this same sense of separation. Take, for example, the veil which Moses had to wear when he came down from Mount Sinai. When God had spoken to Moses on Mount Sinai, the glorious manifestation of the Godhead, the Shekinah Glory, had so vividly stamped itself upon the face of Moses that he had to wear a veil to conceal that glory from the eyes of mortal men. None could stand the presence of that reflected glory, for we read in Exodus 34: 33: "And till Moses had done speaking with them, he put a vail on his face. But when Moses went in before the Lord to speak with him, he took the vail off, until he came out. . . . And the children of Israel saw the face of Moses, that the skin of Moses' face shone: and Moses put the vail upon his face, until he went in to speak with him."

Between the holy, righteous God and sinful men there is this great separation which is signified by Moses' veil, the Veil of the Tabernacle, and later by the Veil in the Temple.

But the Bible tells us of still another veil which signifies this separation. We read in John 1:14 that the Word was made flesh and tabernacled amongst men. Christ's body or flesh was thus a veil which hid His Deity from the eyes of men. Looking upon Christ, men did not see that He was very God of very God. They asked, "Is not this the carpenter's son?" (Mark 6:3) Isaiah, in prophetic vision, foresaw that He would be one of very uncomely visage (Isaiah 52:14).

74

CALVARY ABOLISHED THE SEPARATION

Nevertheless, as we trace the story of our Lord's earthly sojourn and public ministry, we see glimpses of His glory. By divine revelation, His disciples were able to see beyond the veil of His flesh and behold the fact that He was the Son of God. John 1:14 declares that the disciples beheld His glory, the glory as of the only begotten of the Father, full of grace and truth. Glimpses of His glory were manifested to the disciples at the wedding in Cana of Galilee (John 2:1–11). There He changed the water into wine, and John records, "This beginning of miracles did Jesus in Cana of Galilee, and manifested forth his glory; and his disciples believed on him." Other miracles in John's Gospel were moments when glimpses of Christ's glory shone forth through the veil of His flesh. Then turn to Matthew 17:2, where we read concerning the incident on the Mount of Transfiguration that Jesus ". . . was transfigured before them: and his face did shine as the sun, and his raiment was white as the light." Peter, recalling this incident in later life, said, "We . . . were eyewitnesses of his majesty" (II Peter 1:16).

But these glimpses of glory climaxed at the moment when Christ died. Turn in your Bibles to Mark 15:37, 38, and read what happened the moment Christ died on the Cross of Calvary: "And Jesus cried with a loud voice, and gave up the ghost. And the veil of the temple was rent in twain from the top to the bottom." Human might could not have been responsible for tearing this veil, for it was thirty feet wide, thirty feet high, and a handbreadth thick! It was rent by the power of Almighty God! God rent this veil at the very moment when Christ died for the sins of the world on Calvary's Cross. Hence, the gap which once separated the holy, righteous God from sinful, depraved men is now bridged by the finished work of Christ on the Cross. Now those who have entrusted themselves to Christ may have continuous access to the Holy of Holies, and have constant communion and fellowship with God. Hence, we read in Hebrews 10:19, 20 that we may have boldness to enter into the holiest by the blood of Jesus, by a new and living way which he hath consecrated for us, through the veil, that is to say, his flesh.

Thus the glory which emanated from Christ from time to time during His earthly ministry can now be seen continuously after His death and resurrection by all who have repented of their sins and put their faith in Christ. Instead of the one day a year when one man could go into the Holy of Holies, all who have believed in Christ can have constant access to God through Christ Who has entered the Holy of Holies for us and rent the veil which separates by His death on the Cross.

Are you discouraged? Are you weary? Are difficulties coming your way so fast and pressures coming so heavy that you know not which way to turn? Are you at wit's end corner? Well, remember, if you have received Christ as Saviour you can come in prayer boldly, through the rent veil, into the Holy of Holies, pouring out all your problems, sorrow, and heartaches, knowing that His ear is ever open to your cry. He will answer you; He will comfort you; He will undertake in your situation.

Satan tries to keep you from God, tries to make you feel condemned and unworthy. He tries to keep you from the secret place, but God says, "Come! Come! Come! Make your petitions known unto me." The Word says, "In everything by prayer and supplication with thanksgiving, let your requests be made known unto God, and the peace of God which passeth all understanding shall keep your heart and mind in Christ Jesus" (Phillipians 4:6, 7). And we need that assurance, brother, in these days when the enemy is coming in like a flood. We need it.

Let's bow our heads in prayer, no one stirring. Then, though I do not know where my voice is going in the great radio audience, I feel that it is going into homes that have been darkened by Satan, the god of this age. I feel that people have heard this message and are kneeling right now, possibly beside a chair in the kitchen, or in the bedroom, and they are coming to God through Jesus Christ and are saying, "The veil is rent and Heavenly Father, I want to commune with Thee, upon Thy throne." Jesus says, "Come unto me, all ye that labor and are heavy laden and I will give you rest" (Matthew 11: 28). So come now while the door is open and know the full salvation that is in Christ.

CHAPTER IX

The Ark of the Covenant

TODAY WE STEP WITH SPECIAL REVERENCE AND HOLY awe beyond the Veil, the curtain separating the Holy Place from the Holy of Holies, and behold the holiest of all the furnishings of the Tabernacle. We look at that spot which in Old Testament days was the holiest place on earth—the Holy of Holies, where we find the Ark of the Covenant, the Mercy Seat, the Cherubim, and the Shekinah Glory. The reason for this sanctity was that at the Ark of the Covenant God's presence was locally manifest, for we read in Exodus 25:22, "And there I will meet with thee, and I will commune with thee from above the mercy seat, . . ."

You may wonder about the exact meaning of the word "ark." The word carries with it the idea of a chest for the safe-keeping of cherished articles. Thus the Ark contained the two tables of stone on which were written the Ten Commandments, the

golden pot of manna, and Aaron's rod that budded
—articles most cherished because they signified
God's mighty, miraculous deeds on Israel's behalf.

ITS DETAILS PICTURE CHRIST'S PERSON AND WORK

This Ark, or chest, was made of acacia wood,
Exodus 25:10. Acacia wood is a very hard and close-
grained wood which was found in and around Mount
Sinai. Note that God did not command Moses to
make the Ark out of the cedars of Lebanon, or out
of the oak or gopherwood of Palestine, for that
would have meant a long wait while an arduous
journey was made to procure these woods. Instead,
the Lord had them make the Ark out of acacia
wood, the common wood of the desert where they
were encamped. So likewise God did not send us His
Son in the form of an archangel, or in some body be-
longing to another realm; rather, He sent His Son
in the likeness of sinful flesh, to be as a man upon
the earth. Instead of our having to go to Him, God
came to where we are. Being as we are, Christ has
known the sufferings, sorrows, and temptations
which are the lot of our daily life. How wonderful
it is to have as our Mediator One Who has experienced the problems we constantly face!

As for its size, this Ark of the Covenant was
about three feet six inches long, two feet six inches
wide and two feet six inches deep. The acacia wood
of the Ark was overlaid with gold on both its inside

and outside. However, there was no wood in the lid of the Ark, for this was the Mercy Seat, which was made of pure gold. Hence, the Ark was composed of two materials, wood and gold, and this calls to our minds the fact that Christ is both human and divine—He is one Person having both a human and divine nature. The common acacia wood of the desert points to His essential humanity, while the gold points to His Deity. How wonderful to have One as our Mediator Who is also very God of very God!

At both ends of the Mercy Seat there was a Cherub made of gold. These Cherubim faced each other with their wings outstretched, covering the Mercy Seat. Thus they were to be seen looking forward and down, their gaze meeting at the middle of the Mercy Seat. And beloved, this is most significant, because it was on the center of the Mercy Seat that the blood was applied each year when the High Priest entered the Holy of Holies on the Day of Atonement. If the Cherubim's attention was constantly focused upon the shed blood of sacrificial animals in Old Testament times, how much more should our attention be centered upon the Cross, where Christ's blood made atonement for our sins! Like Paul of old we should say, ". . . God forbid that I should glory save in the cross . . . I determine to know anything among you save Jesus Christ and Him crucified" (Galations 6:14; I Corinthians 2:2).

The Shekinah Glory hovered over the Mercy Seat. This Shekinah Glory was a local manifestation of the very presence of God, and since this presence was located between the Cherubim over the place where the shed blood was applied, we see once again the fact that it is impossible to come into the presence of God unless one comes to the Cross of Christ, humbly admitting his sin, his inability to save himself, and trusting completely in the finished work of Christ. For in Exodus 25:22 God says, "And there I will meet with thee, and I will commune with thee from above the mercy seat, from between the two cherubims which are upon the ark of the testimony. . . ." Hence, we can meet and commune with God only at the place where atonement has been made by shed blood.

IT PICTURES GOD'S PRESENCE AND POWER

Having now understood something of the details of the Ark of the Covenant, let us consider what the Ark, including the Mercy Seat and the Cherubim, symbolized to Israel. We can understand this by noting how the presence or absence of the Ark affected the fortunes of Israel.

First of all, let us consider the first real journey of the Ark of the Covenant recorded in Numbers 10:33: "And they departed from the mount of the Lord three days' journey: and the ark of the covenant of the Lord went before them in the three days' journey [how sweet—listen] to search out a resting place for them." While still at Mount Sinai, Moses had said to the Lord that he did not want to continue having the crushing responsibility of leading the children of Israel to the Promised Land unless God's presence continued to go with him to give him rest (Exodus 33:14, 15). God's answer to the need of Moses and the children of Israel was the Ark of the Covenant, which, in conjunction with the fiery, cloudy pillar, was the means by which God's presence went with them to lead them and give them rest. Through His presence in the Ark of the Covenant, God guided Israel through her wilderness journeyings, and thus the Ark points to Christ Who, when He putteth forth His sheep, goes before, and the sheep follow Him, for they know His voice (John 10:4). Today Christ gives rest to those who have entrusted themselves to Him. Friend of mine, do you know the rest and perfect peace that Christ alone can give as He guides you through this troubled world?

But the Ark of the Covenant was also the means by which the power of God was manifested to the children of Israel. Upon arrival at Kadesh-barnea, spies were sent ahead to search out the Promised Land, so that the best strategy for conquering it could be found. However, when the twelve spies returned, ten of them were so despondent with unbelief that they caused all of Israel to be so discouraged

that they refused to follow God to conquer the land.
Thereupon, God decreed that all of the people
above twenty years of age (except Caleb and Joshua)
should die in the wilderness during the thirty-eight
years that they should wander aimlessly without entering Canaan. Stricken with remorse, the people
tried to return and conquer the Amalekites and the
Canaanites. But in Numbers 14:44 we read, ". . .
Nevertheless the ark of the covenant of the Lord
and Moses, departed not out of the camp. Then the
Amalekites came down, and the Canaanites which
dwelt in that hill, and smote them, and discomfited
them, even unto Hormah." They suffered absolute
defeat because the Ark of the Covenant, the means
by which God's presence and power was manifested
to them, did not go with them into battle. Thus the
works which we try to do by our own self-effort will
be the wood, hay, and stubble which will be burned
up at the Judgment Seat of Christ.

But those works done in the power of the Holy
Spirit, through Christ and Christ alone, will stand
the fires of judgment as gold, silver, and precious
stones. So let us see what occurred when the Ark did
go into battle with the children of Israel at the siege
of Jericho. In Joshua 6:6–8, we read how the Ark
of the Covenant went before the children of Israel
as they marched around the walls of Jericho for
seven days. And then on the seventh day came the
blast of the trumpets and the shout of victory, and

the walls of Jericho came down. Amen! Hallelujah, when we walk in God's presence, we are able to know God's power for our lives. Thus Paul could say, "I can do all things through Christ Who strengthened me" (Phillipians 4:13). And so also Christ said, ". . . without me ye can do nothing" (John 15:5).

Friend of mine, do you know God's presence and power in your life? Do you have communion with God through the Person of Jesus Christ, on the basis of His atoning death and resurrection life? Won't you now kneel by your radio there, and ask God to be merciful to you, a sinner, and forgive your sins on the basis of Christ's finished work? Let Christ take over your life so that you may experience the very pleasure and power of God, and know the rest that comes from following Him. Do not put this off; now is the accepted time; now is the day of salvation. Let me know of your decision by writing to me, Charles E. Fuller, P.O. Box 123, Los Angeles, California.

CHAPTER X

The Blood-Sprinkled Mercy Seat

PLEASE TURN IN YOUR BIBLES WITH ME TO EXODUS 25: 17–22. And may I give you this word that if you'll listen carefully and heed the teaching contained herein, I can guarantee that your thinking will never go astray from basic Christian doctrine. The teaching concerning the blood-sprinkled Mercy Seat is basic, foundational, and eternal.

THE REASON FOR ITS GREAT VALUE

Now the Ark of the Covenant located in the Holy of Holies, was shaped like a chest and contained three things: the law of God written on two tables of stone, the golden pot of manna, and Aaron's rod that budded. The covering or lid of this chest was the blood-sprinkled Mercy Seat. Exodus 25:17 declares that it was to be made of pure gold. Thus it had a greater value than the golden Altar of

Incense which was made of wood overlaid with gold. Being made of solid gold, the Mercy Seat's value is estimated to have been around $60,000 in present day value. However the great value of the Mercy Seat lay not in its solid gold. Rather it derived from the shed blood of the sacrificial lamb that was sprinkled upon it yearly on the Day of Atonement. The Overshadowing Cherubim, likewise made of solid gold, and part and parcel with the Mercy Seat itself, were made always to look, not at the pure gold, but at the shed blood sprinkled on the Mercy Seat. (See Exodus 25:20). These Cherubim, guardians of the holiness of God, help us to realize that we are not redeemed with corruptible things as silver and gold, but with the precious blood of Christ (I Peter 1:18, 18). They help us to learn, along with Paul, to know nothing among us save Jesus Christ and Him crucified (I Corinthians 2:2).

A PROPITIATORY COVERING

Let us consider the significance of the word "mercy." The basic meaning of the words "mercy seat" is "propitiatory covering." Since this is a big word but very necessary to help you understand the meaning of the Mercy Seat, it would be well for you to write it on the margin of your Bible opposite Exodus 25:17. This propitiatory covering (Mercy Seat) covered the law, or the Ten Commandments, which were written on two tables of stone and placed inside the Ark of the Covenant.

Now God's wrath is revealed from heaven against all unrighteousness and ungodliness of men (Romans 1:18). God has wrath against sinful men because they have transgressed His law, which is the revelation of His standard of righteousness. Since we are children of wrath by nature (Ephesians 2:3), there would be no hope for us if the way of salvation consisted in living up to God's standard of righteousness as given in the law. Were there no propitiatory covering for our sins, we would all fall immediately into the hands of the Almighty God of wrath.

A good illustration of this truth is to be found in I Samuel, chapter 6. We read that the Philistines had captured the Ark of the Covenant and had carried it away from the children of Israel. Then verse 19 says, ". . . He [God] smote the men of Bethshemesh because they had looked into the ark of the Lord, even He smote of the people fifty thousand and threescore and ten men. . . ." Why had God slain over fifty thousand men? Because some of their number had had the audacity to peer into the Ark and behold the law without the protection of the intervening propitiatory covering!

And the same fate will befall you, my friend, if you try to save yourself by living according to the law, without trusting completely and solely in Christ Who alone kept the law perfectly and Whose shed blood is that which propitiates the wrath of Almighty God. To everyone who seeks to be saved by keeping the law God says, ". . . Cursed is every one that continueth not in all things which are written in the book of the law to do them." (Galatians 3:10) Likewise in James 2:10 he says, "For whosoever shall keep the whole law, and yet offend in one point, he is guilty of all." If you try to save yourself by living according to the law now, you must someday face the God of wrath who will judge you on the basis of that law, and you will be punished by eternal separation.

CHRIST IS OUR PROPITIATORY COVERING

But there is no need for you to make futile efforts to save yourself by the law. It is not necessary that you stand before God as judge and be sentenced to an eternal hell. For we read in Romans 3:25 that God set forth Christ to be a propitiation for our sins. Christ is the propitiatory covering so that no man needs to face the wrath of Almighty God. Again in I John 4:10 we read, ". . . God . . . loved us and sent His Son to be the propitiation for our sins." Also in I John 2:2, we read that Christ is the propitiation for our sins, and not for ours only, but also for the sins of the whole world.

Now you remember the publican's prayer recorded in Luke 18:13. In contrast with the self-righteous Pharisee who had the audacity to think that he had lived up to God's righteous standard of the law, the poor publican with deep humility would not so much as lift up his eyes to heaven but smote his breast saying, "God be *merciful* to me a sinner." That word "merciful" comes from the same word that signifies "Mercy Seat," or "propitiatory covering." Hence what the publican really meant when he said this was, "God be a propitiatory covering for me who is a sinner."

Our own righteousness is as filthy rags, but if we take Christ to be our propitiatory covering we will be clothed in the bridal dress of His righteousness. (Isaiah 61:10). So kneel down by your radio there, sinning friend of mine, and pray the publican's prayer in faith believing: "God, I accept Jesus Christ as my propitiatory covering." Yes, God so loved the world that He gave His only begotten Son that whosoever believeth in Him should not perish but have everlasting life. There is no need for you to face the wrath of God at the judgment of the great white throne, for God has provided a propitiatory covering for your sins in the person of His Son Jesus Christ. The door of salvation is still open; why will you wait, dear brother? Now is the day of salvation, now is the accepted time! So come and accept God's merciful provision for you!

CHAPTER XI

The Pillar of Cloud and Fire

PLEASE PICTURE WITH ME A NATION OF PEOPLE, ONE
million five hundred thousand strong—men, women and children, with their personal belongings
and cattle leaving Egypt where they had been dwelling for some 400 years. God had appointed Moses
to lead this vast throng as they headed toward the
Promised Land of Canaan. And remember, my
friend, they were going by paths which to them
were absolutely unknown! How would they be
guided? How would they be protected? How would
they be sheltered from the cruel and devastating
desert sandstorms and heat? What provision would
there be for light during the long, dark desert night?
Ah, God who is ever faithful, provided for His children the pillar of cloud by day and the pillar of fire
by night. And best of all *He went before*—He led

them! Read Exodus 13:21, 22: "And the Lord went before them by day in a pillar of cloud, to lead them in the way; . . . by night in a pillar of fire, to give them light; to go by day and night: He took not away the pillar of cloud by day, nor the pillar of fire by night, from before the people." Truly God is faithful!

Four hundred years before this exodus from Egypt, Israel had left their homeland on account of a severe famine. They had traveled south and west, going some 300 miles to the land of Goshen, to the rich and fertile delta regions of the River Nile. There they had suffered long years of slavery under cruel task masters. And now, after four hundred years, Israel was leaving, traveling eastward toward the Red Sea. Look at your map in the back of your Bible, and follow the journey of the children of Israel.

GOD'S PROVISION FOR GUIDANCE

Notice Exodus 13:17: "And it came to pass when Pharoah had let the people go, that God led them not through the way of the land of the Philistines, [that land lying on the shores of the Mediterranean Sea between Egypt and Canaan] although that was near; for God said, lest peradventure the people repent when they see war and they return to Egypt. But God led the people about, through the way of the wilderness of the Red Sea. . . ." Please underline those words "But God" and wherever you find those two words linked together in the Bible just pause and consider them, for the Holy Spirit will enlighten you, and you will see new truth.

Now God provided that pillar of cloud by day and pillar of fire by night, but what was its origin? That remains a mystery. We are not told how it came into being—only *when* it came. Please note that it was a pillar, not just a hovering cloud, but a pillar of cloud, and a pillar indicates strength. That great company of people fleeing from Egypt had great need of strength—God's strength—on that dark night, for they were being pursued by the Egyptians with great numbers of chariots, horses, and horsemen. They were in a dangerous spot: they were fleeing through a gap between two mountains with the Red Sea in front of them and this hostile army led by Pharaoh behind them. He doubtless thought that Israel was an easy prey, entangled in the land. From outward appearance it looked as though God were leading Israel to her doom. But wait! God was leading Israel to a place of blessing, and He was leading Pharaoh and the Egyptians to a place of destruction in the Red Sea. What happened? It was here that the pillar of cloud by day and the pillar of fire by night appeared—God's loving provision for the protection of His children. Read with me Exodus 14:19, 20: "And the angel of God, which went before the camp of Israel, removed and went behind them: and the pillar of . . . cloud went from before their face, and stood behind them: and it came between the camp of the Egyptians and the camp of Israel; and it was a cloud and darkness to them, but it gave light by night to these so that the one came not near the other all night."

Oh, Israel was fearful and complaining, wishing they had remained in bondage in Egypt. But Moses said to the people, "Fear not, stand firm and see the salvation of the Lord which he shall work for you today. For the Egyptians whom you see today you shall never see again. The Lord will fight for you and you have only to be still." Then God spoke to Moses and said, "Lift up your rod and stretch out your hand over the sea and divide it that the children of Israel may go on dry ground through the sea." Then a strong east wind blew all night long and divided the waters so there was a wall of water on each side as the children of Israel passed through on a dry path. Then the pillar of cloud and fire which had gone behind the children of Israel (a light to them, but darkness to the Egyptians) went before to lead them. God provided this cloud for a protection, a guide and a light. Oh, I am so glad, that personally speaking, I have the pillar of cloud and the pillar of fire, the Lord Jesus to stand between me and the god of this age, Satan, who hates the righteous.

THE NECESSITY OF OBEYING GOD

As the cloud moved on, Israel was led to the beautiful shade of the seventy palm trees and the wonderful water from the twelve wells of Elim. No doubt they wanted to remain at Elim, but no, God led His dear children along with the pillar of cloud to guide them, God working out His perfect will for His Own as they followed in submission. He leads those who are obedient, those who are willing to follow. Remember this when you sing, "Where He Leads Me I Will Follow," and associate it with the pillar of fire and the pillar of cloud.

Now the pillar of fire by night gave light. Note, please, that Israel was in the Wilderness. This great caravan included one million five-hundred thousand people on that arduous journey, yet this pillar of fire stood at the Red Sea and flood-lighted the path that God made through the Sea, with walls of water on each side, but it darkened the way of the Egyptians. It is nighttime now. Paul speaks of the night being far spent. Satan, the god of this age, and his army of wicked hosts, are not on our trail. We need light. But God's Word is a pillar of light in the night season to us, a lamp unto our feet and a light unto our path. The entrance of God's Word gives light. Do you need light on your perplexing problems, my brother? Go to the Word and God will give you the answer. He never fails.

95

Not only was that pillar of fire a light, but it was a pillar of cloud by day, a great umbrella over the entire camp of Israel, protecting them from the burning heat of the desert sun. Then, when the night shadows began to fall, God's children could see that pillar of cloud gradually transformed, transfused, changed into a pillar of fire. I wish I could have seen it! What an awesome sight it must have been, and yet how glorious! I wish I could have stood there in the great desert wastes to watch that great umbrella over those hosts of people gradually change. How it must have comforted and cheered those weary travelers to be constantly reminded of God's protection and love as they beheld that cloud.

The Psalmist speaks of this in Psalm 105:39: "He [Jehovah] spread a cloud for a covering: and fire to give light in the night." So, "The sun shall not smite thee by day nor the moon by night." Again, in Psalm 91: "He that dwelleth in the secret place of the most high shall abide under the shadow of the Almighty."

Oh friend of mine, outside of Christ, do you need a pillar of fire by night and a pillar of cloud by day to guide and protect you until you finish this pilgrim journey? While our heads are bowed, will you make the great decision today, will you? Entrust yourself to Christ so He may become your constant guide throughout this life on earth.